HAL•LEONARD

INSTRUMENTAL PLAY-ALONG

AUDIO ACCESS INCLUDED

PLAYBACK+
Speed • Pitch • Balance • Loop

TRUMPET

T0083348

HIT SONGS

Audio arrangements by Peter Deneff

To access audio, visit:
www.halleonard.com/mylibrary

Enter Code
6660-6497-6231-5129

ISBN 978-1-70515-012-2

HAL•LEONARD®

Visit Hal Leonard Online at
www.halleonard.com

Contact us:
Hal Leonard
7777 West Bluemound Road
Milwaukee, WI 53213
Email: info@halleonard.com

In Europe, contact:
Hal Leonard Europe Limited
42 Wigmore Street
Marylebone, London, W1U 2RN
Email: info@halleonardeurope.com

In Australia, contact:
Hal Leonard Australia Pty. Ltd.
4 Lentara Court
Cheltenham, Victoria, 3192 Australia
Email: info@halleonard.com.au

CONTENTS

4

ADORE YOU

TRUMPET

Words and Music by HARRY STYLES,
THOMAS HULL, TYLER JOHNSON
and AMY ALLEN

ANYONE

TRUMPET

Words and Music by JUSTIN BIEBER,
JON BELLION, JORDAN JOHNSON,
ALEXANDER IZQUIERDO, ANDREW WATT,
RAUL CUBINA, STEFAN JOHNSON
and MICHAEL POLLACK

BAD HABITS

TRUMPET

Words and Music by ED SHEERAN,
JOHNNY McDAID and FRED GIBSON

BANG!

TRUMPET

Words and Music by ADAM METZGER,
JACK METZGER and RYAN METZGER

BLINDING LIGHTS

TRUMPET

Words and Music by ABEL TESFAYE,
MAX MARTIN, JASON QUENNEVILLE,
OSCAR HOLTER and AHMAD BALSHE

CIRCLES

TRUMPET

Words and Music by AUSTIN POST,
KAAN GUNESBERK, LOUIS BELL,
WILLIAM WALSH and ADAM FEENEY

11

To Coda $\oplus$

mf

D.S. al Coda

CODA $\oplus$

DRIVERS LICENSE

TRUMPET

Words and Music by OLIVIA RODRIGO
and DANIEL NIGRO

HEATHER

TRUMPET

Words and Music by
CONAN GRAY

THEREFORE I AM

TRUMPET

Words and Music by BILLIE EILISH O'CONNELL
and FINNEAS O'CONNELL

KINGS & QUEENS

TRUMPET

Words and Music by DESMOND CHILD,
AMANDA KOCI, BRETT McLAUGHLIN,
HENRY WALTER, MADISON LOVE,
HILLARY BERNSTEIN, JAKOB ERIXSON,
MIMOZA BLINSON and NADIR KHAYAT

17

D.S. al Coda

CODA

SEÑORITA

TRUMPET

Words and Music by CAMILA CABELLO,
CHARLOTTE AITCHISON, JACK PATTERSON,
SHAWN MENDES, MAGNUS HØIBERG,
BENJAMIN LEVIN, ALI TAMPOSI
and ANDREW WOTMAN

Moderately

Muted Guitar

To Coda ⊕ | 1.

2.
f

1.

2.

D.S. al Coda
(no repeat)

CODA
⊕

f

1.

2.

WILLOW

TRUMPET

Words and Music by TAYLOR SWIFT
and AARON DESSNER

WITHOUT YOU

TRUMPET

Words and Music by BLAKE SLATKIN,
OMER FEDI, BILLY WALSH
and CHARLTON HOWARD

Moderately, in 2

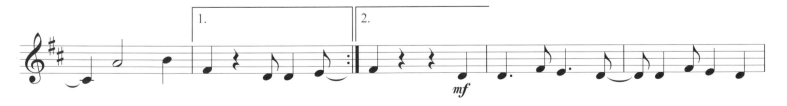

12 Hot Singles

Broken (lovelytheband) • Havana (Camila Cabello) • Heaven (Kane Brown) • High Hopes (Panic! At the Disco) • The Middle (Zedd, Maren Morris & Grey) • Natural (Imagine Dragons) • No Place like You (Backstreet Boys) • Shallow (Lady Gaga & Bradley Cooper) • Sucker (Jonas Brothers) • Sunflower (Post Malone & Swae Lee) • thank u, next (Ariana Grande) • Youngblood (5 Seconds of Summer).

___	00298576	Flute	$14.99
___	00298577	Clarinet	$14.99
___	00298578	Alto Sax	$14.99
___	00298579	Tenor Sax	$14.99
___	00298580	Trumpet	$14.99
___	00298581	Horn	$14.99
___	00298582	Trombone	$14.99
___	00298583	Violin	$14.99
___	00298584	Viola	$14.99
___	00298585	Cello	$14.99

12 Pop Hits

Believer • Can't Stop the Feeling • Despacito • It Ain't Me • Look What You Made Me Do • Million Reasons • Perfect • Send My Love (To Your New Lover) • Shape of You • Slow Hands • Too Good at Goodbyes • What About Us.

___	00261790	Flute	$12.99
___	00261791	Clarinet	$12.99
___	00261792	Alto Sax	$12.99
___	00261793	Tenor Sax	$12.99
___	00261794	Trumpet	$12.99
___	00261795	Horn	$12.99
___	00261796	Trombone	$12.99
___	00261797	Violin	$12.99
___	00261798	Viola	$12.99
___	00261799	Cello	$12.99

Classic Rock

Don't Fear the Reaper • Fortunate Son • Free Fallin' • Go Your Own Way • Jack and Diane • Money • Old Time Rock & Roll • Sweet Home Alabama • 25 or 6 to 4 • and more.

___	00294356	Flute	$14.99
___	00294357	Clarinet	$14.99
___	00294358	Alto Sax	$14.99
___	00294359	Tenor Sax	$14.99
___	00294360	Trumpet	$14.99
___	00294361	Horn	$14.99
___	00294362	Trombone	$14.99
___	00294363	Violin	$14.99
___	00294364	Viola	$14.99
___	00294365	Cello	$14.99

Contemporary Broadway

Defying Gravity (from Wicked) • Michael in the Bathroom (from Be More Chill) • My Shot (from Hamilton) • Seize the Day (from Newsies) • She Used to Be Mine (from Waitress) • Stupid with Love (from Mean Girls) • Waving Through a Window (from Dear Evan Hansen) • When I Grow Up (from Matilda) • and more.

___	00298704	Flute	$14.99
___	00298705	Clarinet	$14.99
___	00298706	Alto Sax	$14.99
___	00298707	Tenor Sax	$14.99
___	00298708	Trumpet	$14.99
___	00298709	Horn	$14.99
___	00298710	Trombone	$14.99
___	00298711	Violin	$14.99
___	00298712	Viola	$14.99
___	00298713	Cello	$14.99

Disney Movie Hits

Beauty and the Beast • Belle • Circle of Life • Cruella De Vil • Go the Distance • God Help the Outcasts • Hakuna Matata • If I Didn't Have You • Kiss the Girl • Prince Ali • When She Loved Me • A Whole New World.

___	00841420	Flute	$12.99
___	00841421	Clarinet	$12.99
___	00841422	Alto Sax	$12.99
___	00841423	Trumpet	$12.99
___	00841424	French Horn	$12.99
___	00841425	Trombone/Baritone	$12.99
___	00841426	Violin	$12.99
___	00841427	Viola	$12.99
___	00841428	Cello	$12.99
___	00841686	Tenor Sax	$12.99
___	00841687	Oboe	$12.99

Disney Solos

Be Our Guest • Can You Feel the Love Tonight • Colors of the Wind • Friend like Me • Part of Your World • Under the Sea • You'll Be in My Heart • You've Got a Friend in Me • Zero to Hero • and more.

___	00841404	Flute	$12.99
___	00841405	Clarinet/Tenor Sax	$12.99
___	00841406	Alto Sax	$12.99
___	00841407	Horn	$12.99
___	00841408	Trombone/Baritone	$12.99
___	00841409	Trumpet	$12.99
___	00841410	Violin	$12.99
___	00841411	Viola	$12.99
___	00841412	Cello	$12.99
___	00841506	Oboe	$12.99
___	00841553	Mallet Percussion	$12.99

Great Classical Themes

Blue Danube Waltz (Strauss) • Can Can (from Orpheus in the Underworld) (Offenbach) • Jesu, Joy of Man's Desiring (J.S. Bach) • Morning Mood (from Peer Gynt) (Grieg) • Ode to Joy (from Symphony No. 9) (Beethoven) • William Tell Overture (Rossini) • and more.

___	00292727	Flute	$12.99
___	00292728	Clarinet	$12.99
___	00292729	Alto Sax	$12.99
___	00292730	Tenor Sax	$12.99
___	00292732	Trumpet	$12.99
___	00292733	Horn	$12.99
___	00292735	Trombone	$12.99
___	00292736	Violin	$12.99
___	00292737	Viola	$12.99
___	00292738	Cello	$12.99

The Greatest Showman

Come Alive • From Now On • The Greatest Show • A Million Dreams • Never Enough • The Other Side • Rewrite the Stars • This Is Me • Tightrope.

___	00277389	Flute	$14.99
___	00277390	Clarinet	$14.99
___	00277391	Alto Sax	$14.99
___	00277392	Tenor Sax	$14.99
___	00277393	Trumpet	$14.99
___	00277394	Horn	$14.99
___	00277395	Trombone	$14.99
___	00277396	Violin	$14.99
___	00277397	Viola	$14.99
___	00277398	Cello	$14.99

Irish Favorites

Danny Boy • I Once Loved a Lass • The Little Beggarman • The Minstrel Boy • My Wild Irish Rose • The Wearing of the Green • and dozens more!

___	00842489	Flute	$12.99
___	00842490	Clarinet	$12.99
___	00842491	Alto Sax	$12.99
___	00842493	Trumpet	$12.99
___	00842494	Horn	$12.99
___	00842495	Trombone	$12.99
___	00842496	Violin	$12.99
___	00842497	Viola	$12.99
___	00842498	Cello	$12.99

Simple Songs

All of Me • Evermore • Hallelujah • Happy • I Gotta Feeling • I'm Yours • Lava • Rolling in the Deep • Viva la Vida • You Raise Me Up • and more.

___	00249081	Flute	$12.99
___	00249082	Clarinet	$12.99
___	00249083	Alto Sax	$12.99
___	00249084	Tenor Sax	$12.99
___	00249086	Trumpet	$12.99
___	00249087	Horn	$12.99
___	00249089	Trombone	$12.99
___	00249090	Violin	$12.99
___	00249091	Viola	$12.99
___	00249092	Cello	$12.99
___	00249093	Oboe	$12.99
___	00249094	Keyboard Percussion	$12.99

Stadium Rock

Crazy Train • Don't Stop Believin' • Eye of the Tiger • Havana • Seven Nation Army • Sweet Caroline • We Are the Champions • and more.

___	00323880	Flute	$14.99
___	00323881	Clarinet	$14.99
___	00323882	Alto Sax	$14.99
___	00323883	Tenor Sax	$14.99
___	00323884	Trumpet	$14.99
___	00323885	Horn	$14.99
___	00323886	Trombone	$14.99
___	00323887	Violin	$14.99
___	00323888	Viola	$14.99
___	00323889	Cello	$14.99

Video Game Music

Angry Birds • Assassin's Creed III • Assassin's Creed Revelations • Battlefield 1942 • Civilization IV (Baba Yetu) • Deltarune (Don't Forget) • Elder Scrolls IV & V • Fallout® 4 • Final Fantasy VII • Full Metal Alchemist (Bratja) (Brothers) • IL-2 Sturmovik: Birds of Prey • Splinter Cell: Conviction • Undertale (Megalovania).

___	00283877	Flute	$12.99
___	00283878	Clarinet	$12.99
___	00283879	Alto Sax	$12.99
___	00283880	Tenor Sax	$12.99
___	00283882	Trumpet	$12.99
___	00283883	Horn	$12.99
___	00283884	Trombone	$12.99
___	00283885	Violin	$12.99
___	00283886	Viola	$12.99
___	00283887	Cello	$12.99

HAL•LEONARD®